Twitter For Absolute Beginners

A Concise User Guide to Mastering Twitter with Tips and Tricks

Zara Greenwood

Contents

Twitter Follow & Followers

Twitter Following:

How to Follow Someone:

Who should I Follow on Twitter?

Following Counts:

Twitter's Recommendation Algorithm

How many accounts should a new user follow?

Twitter Followers:

Twitter Accounts to Avoid:

INTRODUCTION

This is the definitive guide for anyone eager to dive into the exciting world of Twitter and unlock its endless possibilities. Whether you're a total novice to social media or simply new to Twitter, this book is your essential companion in navigating the platform and harnessing its power to connect, engage, and share your voice with the world.

This comprehensive guide will walk you through every step of your Twitter journey, from creating your account and setting up your profile to mastering the art of tweeting, retweeting, and building a vibrant online presence. With easy-to-follow instructions, practical tips, and real-world examples, you'll quickly grasp the core features and discover the best practices to maximize your Twitter experience.

Uncover the secrets of crafting compelling tweets that captivate your audience and learn how to engage with others through likes, comments, and direct messages. Understand how to leverage hashtags, trending topics, and Twitter chats to expand your reach and connect with like-minded individuals. Plus, discover invaluable strategies to build a loyal following, boost your personal brand, and network with influencers in your industry.

Whether you're using Twitter for personal expression, professional networking, or business promotion, "Twitter for Absolute Beginners" equips you with the knowledge and confidence to navigate the platform like a pro. Get ready to join the vibrant Twitterverse and unlock a world of endless connections, conversations, and opportunities. Let's embark on this exciting journey together and unleash the power of your tweets!

CHAPTER ONE

History of Twitter

Twitter was founded by Jack Dorsey, Biz Stone, and Evan Williams in March 2006. The idea for the platform originated from Dorsey, who envisioned a service that would allow users to share short status updates with their followers.

Initially, the project was named **"twttr"** before evolving into the now well-known name, Twitter. Ever since it has evolved, it has included several features that interest people from all walks of life.

How it First Began:

On March 21, 2006, the founders sent the first tweet, and Twitter was officially launched to the public in July of the same year. At the time, sharing real-time updates was a novelty, and Twitter quickly gained attention and popularity.

As users joined the platform, Twitter's growth accelerated. Celebrities, news organizations, and ordinary individuals flocked to Twitter to share their thoughts, promote their work, and engage with others. The platform's simplicity and the 140 characters per tweet limit encouraged concise communication and made it easy to follow and participate in conversations.

Popularity of Twitter:

Twitter gained significant visibility during major events like the 2007 South by Southwest (SXSW) festival, which was pivotal in coordinating activities and sharing real-time updates. This event catapulted Twitter into the mainstream, expanding its user base rapidly.

Over time, Twitter introduced new features to enhance the user experience. The addition of hashtags in 2007 allowed users to tag their tweets and make them discoverable by others interested in similar topics. The introduction of the retweet function in 2009 made it easier to share other users' tweets with one's own followers, fostering viral trends and amplifying important messages.

Twitter's growth was further propelled by its mobile app, making it accessible to users on smartphones and tablets. The platform became synonymous with instant updates, breaking news, and live commentary during major events like sports matches, award shows, and political debates.

As Twitter continued to evolve, it expanded its offerings by integrating multimedia content, allowing users to share photos, videos, and links. The platform also introduced features such as Twitter Moments, Periscope live streaming, and the ability to poll followers, further enriching the user experience.

Today, Twitter boasts millions of active users, ranging from individuals to businesses and organizations. It has become an integral part of global conversations, a platform for news dissemination, and a medium for individuals to express their thoughts, connect with like-minded people, and engage with public figures.

The journey of Twitter from its humble beginnings to its current status as a global social media phenomenon showcases its enduring impact on communication and information sharing. With its real-time nature and ability to connect people from all walks of life, Twitter has transformed the way we interact and stay informed in the digital age.

Twitter Sales and Takeover:

On April 4, 2022, Elon Musk, the CEO of Tesla and SpaceX, made an unsolicited offer to buy Twitter for \$54.20 per share, or \$44 billion in total. Musk said that he wanted to make Twitter a **"platform for free speech around the globe."**

Twitter's board of directors initially resisted Musk's offer, but after Musk threatened to launch a hostile takeover, they agreed to sell the company to him for \$54.20 per share on April 25, 2022.

Musk's takeover of Twitter has been met with mixed reactions. Some people believe that he will be a positive force for the company, while others are concerned that he will use Twitter to spread misinformation and hate speech.

Here are some of the implications of Musk's takeover of Twitter:

1. **Changes to Twitter's content moderation policies:** Musk has been critical of Twitter's content moderation policies, which he believes are too restrictive. He has said that he wants to make Twitter a "**platform for free speech**," which could lead to changes in the way that the platform handles hate speech, misinformation, and other forms of harmful content.

2. **Changes to Twitter's business model:** Musk has also said that he wants to make Twitter a more profitable company. He has suggested that he could do this by introducing new features, such as paid subscriptions,

or by selling advertising space.

3. **Changes to Twitter's culture:** Musk has a reputation for being a demanding boss. It is possible that his takeover of Twitter could lead to changes in the company's culture, as Musk seeks to impose his own vision for the platform.

It is too early to say what the long-term impact of Musk's takeover of Twitter will be. However, it is clear that his ownership of the platform will have a major impact on the way that it operates.

What Elon Musk Want With Twitter:

In a statement released after the takeover announcement, Musk said, *"Free speech is the bedrock of a functioning democracy, and Twitter is the digital town square where matters vital to the future of humanity are debated."*

This aligns with his previously expressed sentiments over Twitter policies and freedom of speech. He said, *"I also want to make Twitter better than ever by enhancing the product with new features, making the algorithms open source to increase trust, defeating the spam bots, and authenticating all humans."*

CHAPTER TWO
Getting Started

Twitter, as it is today, has come a long way from what the founders first imagined. The user interface has undergone several innovations, and many features have been added and removed to ensure a better user experience.

Features of Twitter

Here are some of the more interesting features on Twitter:

Homepage: This is the page you see when you sign in to your Twitter account. It contains content from people you follow, the content they like or retweet, and personalized content based on your searches and preferences.

Follows: This is a feature that allows you to select your network. Follow friends and people you know to keep up with their updates. If you don't want to miss a person's content, you should also turn on the notification bell.

Tweets: These are short posts made on Twitter. They are often in text format but may contain pictures or videos. For regular Tweets, the character limit is 280. However, if you are a Twitter Blue subscriber, you can tweet up to 4,000 characters.

In addition to making posts/tweets, you can engage with other people's tweets in several ways:

1. Like: this is one of the major metrics for engagement on Twitter.

2. Retweet/Quotes: this feature allows you to share someone else's tweet either exactly as posted in your timeline.

3. Comment: You can also comment on anybody's tweet even if you don't follow the person.

Threads: While tweets are restricted to 280 characters, you can put up much longer content by linking a series of tweets to form a thread. A thread can contain as much as 25 tweets.

Messages: You can also chat one on one with other Twitter users via the message feature. Here, you can chat more expansively as the character limit is pegged at 10000. Messages can also include pictures, gifs, and videos.

Spaces: This audio conferencing feature allows Twitter users to hold meetings. There is no limit to how many people can join a space, but only 13 people can speak simultaneously, including the host and co-hosts. Anyone can join your space, via a shared link.

Twitter Blue: Twitter Blue is a subscription service offered by Twitter that provides users with a variety of features and benefits. These features include:

- **Ad-free browsing:** Twitter Blue subscribers can browse Twitter without seeing ads.

- **Custom emoji:** Twitter Blue subscribers can create and use their own custom emoji.

- **Undo tweets:** Twitter Blue subscribers can undo tweets that they have just posted.

- **Bookmark folders:** Twitter Blue subscribers can create and organize bookmark folders to save their favorite tweets.

- **Color themes:** Twitter Blue subscribers can choose from a variety of color themes to customize the look of their Twitter experience.

- **Communities:** Twitter Blue subscribers can create and join communities, which are groups of people with similar interests.

Downloading Twitter from the Play Store:

Open the Google Play Store: On your Android device, locate the Google Play Store app.

Search for Twitter: Tap the search bar at the top of the Play Store interface and type "**Twitter**" into the search field.

Select the Twitter app: From the search results, look for the official Twitter app. It should have the blue Twitter logo. Tap on it to open the app page.

Install the app: On the Twitter app page, tap the "**Install**" button. You may be prompted to review and accept the app permissions. Once you've read and accepted the permissions, the app will begin downloading and installing on your device.

Downloading Twitter from the Apple App Store:

Open the App Store: On your iOS device, locate the App Store app on your home screen.

Search for Twitter: Tap the search icon at the bottom of the App Store interface and enter "Twitter" in the search field.

Select the Twitter app: From the search results, find the official Twitter app with the blue Twitter logo. Tap on it to view the app page.

Install the app: On the Twitter app page, tap the "**Get**" button, which will change to "**Install**." You will be prompted, provide your Apple ID password or Face ID to authenticate the download.

Signing Up on Twitter:

Signing up for Twitter is a straightforward process. Here's a step-by-step guide on how to create a Twitter account:

- **Open Twitter App:** Proceed to the Twitter app on your device. Alternatively, you can go to your preferred browser and enter the following address (www.twitter.com) in the address bar.

- **Create Account:** If this is your first time of using twitter, you can select the "**Create Account**" button. If you already have a twitter account, you can select "**Login**." Follow the prompt to enter you username and password.

- **Choose a username:** Next, you'll need to enter a unique username, as well as your phone number/email and your date of birth. If you enter a username that has already been used, Twitter will notify you to choose a different name.

Create your account

Name

50

Phone number or email address

Date of birth

Next

- **Verification Code:** Twitter will send a verification code to the number or email you entered during registration. Ensure to enter the sent code to your mobile or email correctly.

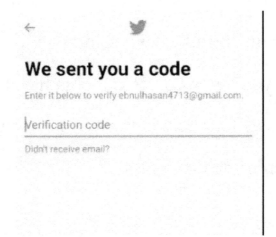

- **Create a password:** Select a strong password that includes a combination of letters, numbers, and symbols. Make sure it's something secure and memorable.

You'll need a password

Make sure it's 8 characters or more.

Password

- **Customize your experience:** After creating a password, you can follow the on-screen prompt to complete the signup process. Here, you will be able to customize your profile, content you see as well as your interest.

CHAPTER THREE

Twitter Profile

Twitter is one of the best social platforms to interact, follow trends, catch up with friends and family, and get news at your fingertip. In this chapter, you will learn how to update your Twitter profile.

Updating Twitter Profile:

Updating your Twitter profile is a great way to personalize your account and make it reflect your interests and personality. Here's a step-by-step guide on how to update your Twitter profile:

1. **Log in to your Twitter account:** Open

the twitter app on your device. Alternatively, you can visit www.twitter.com using any browser app on your device.

2. **Access your profile settings:** Once you're logged in, click on your "**Profile**" icon.

3. **Profile:** Ensure to select "**Profile**" from the options

4. **Edit Profile:** On your profile page, select "**Edit Profile.**"

Here, you can edit the following:

- **Twitter Header:** The header is the first thing people see when they visit your profile. so many users choose an image that represents their personal brand, or personality. Click on the plus on the header, and then choose a new image. Adjust the image as needed, and click "**Save**" to update it.

- **Profile Photo:** The profile photo is often called an avatar, or twitter profile pic. A profile photo can be a picture of you, a logo, an icon, or any image representing you. Click on the plus on the profile photo, and choose an image of yourself.

- **Display Name:** The display name appears

at the top of your profile and next to each of your tweets. It doesn't have to be unique; multiple users can have the same display name. You can change your display name by entering your desired name.

- **Edit Bio:** Your Twitter bio is a way to introduce yourself to other Twitter users and let them know what they can expect from your tweets. You can include personal details, professional information, your interests, etc. In this section, you can write a brief description about yourself or any information you'd like to share.

- **Location:** This is where you can indicate your geographic location. This can be as specific as your city or town, or as general as your country, a region, or even something fictional. The location field is entirely up to you.

- **Website:** This field allows you to link to a website associated with you or your brand. This could be a personal blog, website link, LinkedIn profile, YouTube channel, or any URL that you want to share with your followers.

- **Birth Date:** This is a field where you can optionally share your birthday. You can choose to show the full date (month, day, and year), or you can choose to only show the month and day.

- **Edit Professional Profile:** This is where you can specify the exact profession or business that you are into. You can enter specific information and customize your business directly on your profile.

- **Review and save your changes:** After making all the desired updates, review your profile to ensure everything is accurate and reflects your intended changes. Once you're satisfied, click the **Save** to record your profile updates.

Profile Tips:

Customizing your Twitter profile can help you create an attractive and compelling online presence. Here are some tips to help you customize your Twitter profile effectively:

1. **Profile Picture:** Use a clear and high-quality profile picture that represents your personal brand or the image you want to portray. It can be a professional headshot, a logo, or an image that reflects your interests.

2. **Header Image:** The header image is the large banner at the top of your profile. Choose a visually appealing image that complements your profile picture and aligns with your brand or interests. It could be a beauti-

ful landscape, a relevant graphic, or a photo that represents your niche.

3. **Bio:** Craft a concise and engaging bio that highlights your expertise, interests, or passions. Use keywords that are relevant to your personal brand or the topics you frequently discuss. This can be hashtags that indicate your involvement in specific topics.

4. **Pinned Tweet:** Pin a tweet to the top of your profile that showcases your best work, an important announcement, or a tweet that represents your brand. This helps visitors quickly understand your value or message.

5. **Be Authentic:** Show your personality and be genuine in your tweets. Let your voice and

unique style shine through. People are more likely to follow and engage with accounts that are authentic and relatable.

6. **Engage with Others:** Actively participate in conversations, retweet interesting content, and reply to other users' tweets. Engaging with others helps build connections, expand your network, and increase your profile's visibility.

Remember, customization should align with your personal or professional brand and reflect your unique identity. By applying these tips and adding your own creative flair, you can create an attractive and compelling Twitter profile.

CHAPTER FOUR

Twitter Interface

The interface of Twitter is key to understanding the platform effectively. In this chapter, you will learn how about Twitter interface and how to navigate the different aspect of twitter.

Understanding Twitter Interface:

Twitter has different navigation elements and they are as follow:

(1) Home Feed:

Twitter's home feed displays tweets from the accounts you are following, including their tweets, retweets, likes, replies, etc. The feed also incorporates Twitter's algorithms, which curate content that Twitter believes you will be interested in based on your past interactions. Twitter has two ways to view your Home feed:

For You: Twitter uses an algorithm to show you tweets that will be most relevant to your interests. These can include popular tweets from those you follow, tweets they've liked, and tweets from accounts that you don't follow but are popular in your network.

Following: This view shows you the most recent tweets from the accounts you follow, in chronological order. You won't see any tweets from accounts you don't follow except they retweeted the tweet.

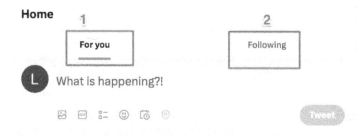

You can toggle between these two views in your twitter home feeds.

(2) Twitter Composer:

The Tweet Composer is where you can compose and share your tweets. You can usually access the Twitter Composer by clicking on the **compose button** in the bottom right corner.

If you use a web browser to access your Twitter account, you'll find the tweet composer at the top of your Home Feed or on the side of your profile page. Once you open the composer, you'll see a large text field. This is where you type the content of your tweet. Twitter has a character limit of 280 characters per tweet.

(3) Notifications:

Twitter Notifications are alerts that keep you updated about activities related to your account. They are typically located in the bell-shaped tab on both the web and mobile versions of Twitter.

Notifications can inform you about several types of activities, including:

- **Mentions:** When other users mention your handle (i.e., @yourusername) in their tweets.

- **Retweets:** When someone retweets (shares) your tweets to their followers.

- **Likes:** When other users like your tweets.

- **Replies:** When users comment on your

tweets.

- **New followers:** When you gain new followers.

- **Direct Messages:** When you receive new direct messages (private messages between you and another user).

(4) Messages:

The Messages or Direct Messages (DMs) feature enables private conversations between users. You can send and receive messages to individuals or groups. Access your messages by clicking on the envelope icon at the top right corner of the interface.

(5) Profile:

Your profile represents your personal or brand identity on Twitter. It displays your profile picture, header image, bio, and a timeline of your tweets. Clicking on your profile picture or the profile icon takes you to your profile page, where you can customize your settings, view your tweets, and manage your account.

(6) Lists:

Lists allow you to curate and organize accounts you follow into specific groups. You can create lists based on topics, interests, or any other criteria you choose. Access your lists by clicking on your profile picture, selecting "**Lists**," and managing or viewing them from there.

(7) Trends:

The Trends section displays the most popular hashtags, topics, and conversations happening on Twitter at a given moment. It helps you stay informed about current events, viral discussions.

(8) Search:

The search bar at the top of the interface enables you to search for specific accounts, hashtags, or keywords. Use it to find relevant content, explore discussions, or discover new accounts to follow.

By familiarizing yourself with these interface elements, you'll be well-equipped to navigate Twitter, engage with others, and make the most of the platform's features and functionalities.

(9) Space Icon:

The space icon is located at the bottom of the Twitter interface, represented by a microphone. Space is a feature that allows users to participate in live audio conversations.

Users can create and join live conversations in the space section in real time. This means that anyone, even those who do not follow you, can join as a listener.

(10) Communities:

The Communities icon on Twitter is located at the bottom of the Twitter interface. When you click on the Communities icon, you will be taken to a page where you can browse existing communities.

Communities are groups of people who share a common interest, such as a hobby, profession, or passion. Once you join a community, you can start tweeting directly to the community members. Your tweets will only be visible to other members of the community.

(11) More Option:

The More Options icon is represented with your profile picture and can be found at the top left corner of the Twitter interface. After selecting the more option, you will be able to access additional options such as Profile, Twitter Blue, Topics, Bookmarks, List, and Twitter Circle, Professional Tools, Settings and Support.

(12) Profile:

Accessing the profile section allows you to customize various aspects of your Twitter account, such as your profile picture, header image, bio, and pinned tweet.

(13) Twitter Blue:

This is the place where you can sign up for a Twitter Blue subscription. Once you click on the designated icon, you will be able to view the price or cost of Twitter Blue that is applicable to your specific region.

(14) Topics:

The topic section is an important feature that allows you to select your interests. This information is used to tailor the content you see on your feed, including tweets, events, and ads. Additionally, the topics you choose will be displayed publicly on your profile.

(15) Bookmarks:

The bookmark section in Twitter is a useful feature that allows you to save tweets that you want to read later. This section is where you can easily access and manage all the tweets you have bookmarked.

(16) Lists:

Lists are a useful feature on Twitter that enables you to categorize and manage the accounts you follow. Lists can be created based on various criteria such as topics, interests, or any other relevant factors.

(17) Twitter Circle:

Twitter Circle is a feature that allows users to share Tweets with a select group of people, rather than with their entire follower base. When you create a Tweet, you will have the option to share it with your Circle or with your public audience.

(18) Professional Tools:

Professional Tools are a set of features that allow businesses and creators to better manage their presence on Twitter.

(19) Settings & Support:

This is where you can access and customize the settings of your Twitter app.

CHAPTER FIVE
Twitter Follow & Followers

After correctly setting up your Twitter account, you can search for people to follow on Twitter. When you begin to follow people, groups, or an organization, you will start to see their tweets, likes, retweets, and interests. This chapter teaches you how to find and follow individuals, groups and influencers.

Twitter Following:

Twitter Following refers to the act of subscribing to another twitter user's. When you follow someone, their tweets will appear in your Home timeline, meaning you'll see their updates whenever you log into Twitter. This allows you to keep up with the thoughts, news, and insights they share.

How to Follow Someone:

Following someone on Twitter is a straightforward process. Here's how you can do it:

- **Open your Twitter account:** Open the Twitter app or go to www.twitter.com in a web browser and log in to your account.

- **Find the user you want to follow:** You can do this in several ways. If you know the username or their handle (their username that starts with @), you can type it into the search bar at the top of the screen.

- **Go to their profile:** In the search result, click on the "**People**" icon to see the list of people with the name you are searching for. Ensure to select the name or profile photo of the person to navigate to their profile page.

- **Click the Follow button:** On the profile page, you'll see a button that says "**Follow.**" Click this button. Once you've done so, the button will change to say "**Following**," indicating that you are now following this user.

When you follow someone, they get a notification about it. This can facilitate connections as it often prompts the other user to check out your profile and maybe follow you back if they find your content interesting.

The list of accounts you follow is public by default, although you can make your profile private if you prefer. Making your profile private means only those you've approved can see who you're following.

NOTE: If the person you're trying to follow has a private account, you will send them a follow request instead of instantly following them. They will have to approve your request before you can see their tweets.

Who should I Follow on Twitter?

Who you should follow on Twitter largely depends on your interests, needs, and the purpose of your Twitter usage. Here are some general categories to consider:

- **Friends and Family:** This can help you keep up with their latest news and thoughts.

- **Influencers and Celebrities:** If there are influencers, celebrities, or public figures that you admire or are interested in, following them can keep you updated on their latest news and thoughts.

- **News Organizations:** Following reputable news outlets can keep you updated with the latest news and current events.

- **Professionals and Organizations:** If you're using Twitter for professional purposes, following key people and organizations in your industry can be beneficial. It can keep you informed about the latest trends, news, and discussions in your field.

- **Educational Accounts:** There are many accounts that regularly share interesting facts, educational content, or thought-provoking ideas.

- **Interests and Hobbies:** Follow accounts that post content about your hobbies or interests, be it sports teams, crafts, cooking, or anything else you enjoy.

- **Local Businesses and Organizations:** Following these can keep you updated about local events, deals, or news.

- **Advocacy Groups:** If there are causes you care about, following related advocacy groups can keep you informed about ways to get involved and latest developments.

Remember, Twitter is a versatile platform that can be tailored to suit your needs and interests. Don't be afraid to follow, unfollow, and explore to curate your Twitter feed to your liking. The goal is to create a meaningful, enjoyable, and beneficial Twitter experience for yourself.

Following Counts:

The Following count on your Twitter profile indicates the number of other Twitter users you have chosen to follow. This number can provide an indication of your interests, as you're likely to follow accounts that post content relevant to you.

In the **Following** tab on your profile, others can see a list of all the accounts you follow. This list is organized in reverse chronological order, so the accounts you've followed most recently are at the top.

Twitter's Recommendation Algorithm

Twitter web version uses algorithm to recommends certain accounts for you to follow.

The algorithm recommends account based on the following:

- **Contacts:** When you sync your phone and email contacts, Twitter recommends your contacts that have Twitter accounts.

- **Followers:** When you follow someone, twitter can recommend their followers.

- **Location:** Twitter may also make suggestions based on your location or your recent activity on Twitter.

- **Promotion:** Twitter suggestions often include promoted accounts.

Twitter also uses all these algorithms to suggest accounts that you might want to follow. These suggestions are based on a variety of factors including: who you're currently following, who they follow, your past interactions, and your profile information.

Remember that these algorithms are constantly being updated and adjusted to improve user experience, and they may also vary slightly based on your personal settings and the specific product or feature of Twitter you're using.

How many accounts should a new user follow?

As a new user, there is a limit to the number of accounts you can follow daily. This number is 400 for unverified accounts and 1000 for verified accounts. Also, if you follow too many accounts simultaneously, you may be temporarily restricted. The restriction is usually be lifted in an hour.

Twitter Followers:

Twitter followers refers to the other users who have chosen to subscribe to your account. When someone follows you, they'll see your tweets in their Home timeline whenever they log into Twitter. The concept is similar to subscribing to a feed of updates or a newsletter; in this case, the updates are the tweets you post. Here are a few key points about followers on Twitter:

- **Notifications:** You receive a notification when someone new starts following you. You can also see a list of your followers by going to your profile and clicking on "**Followers.**"

- **Follower Count:** The number of followers

you have is displayed on your Twitter profile. This count can serve as a rough indicator of your influence or popularity on Twitter, as more followers mean more people are interested in your tweets.

- **Public vs Private:** If your Twitter account is public, anyone can choose to follow you and they will see your tweets immediately. If your account is set to private (protected), you'll receive a follow request when someone wants to follow you, and you can choose whether to accept or reject this request.

- **Interactions:** Having followers increases the potential for interactions on your tweets. Your followers can like, retweet, reply to, and share your tweets. They can also directly message you if your settings allow for this.

- **Following Back:** When someone follows you, it's your choice whether or not to follow them back. Some people choose to follow back everyone who follows them, while others only follow back certain accounts.

- **Unfollowing:** If a follower decides they no longer want to see your tweets, they can choose to unfollow you. This removes your tweets from their Home timeline.

Remember, gaining followers on Twitter is often a combination of posting interesting content, interacting positively with other users, and being active on the platform.

Twitter Accounts to Avoid:

Twitter is filled with different kinds of users, and recent counts show that millions of them might be bots. There is no general rule of thumb, but here are some types of accounts you should be wary of:

- **Fake Accounts:** Be wary of accounts pretending to be someone or something they're not. For example, accounts impersonating celebrities, brands, or public figures.

- **Spam Accounts:** These are accounts that repeatedly post irrelevant content or links, often advertising scams or questionable products. They usually have few followers and post the same message to many users.

- **Bots:** Bots are automated accounts that don't represent real people. While not all bots are harmful (some are designed to share useful information), many are used for spamming or manipulation.

- **Troll Accounts:** Trolls intentionally post provocative or offensive content to upset others and provoke a response. Following these accounts can lead to a negative experience on the platform.

- **Inactive Accounts:** If an account hasn't tweeted in several months or years, it's probably inactive. Following these accounts won't add much value to your Twitter feed.

- **Accounts Sharing Inappropriate Con-**

tent: This can include explicit adult content, violent content, or content promoting hate speech, discrimination, or harassment.

- **Misinformation and Disinformation Accounts:** These are accounts that consistently share unverified, false, or misleading information.

- **Accounts that Violate Twitter's Rules:** This includes accounts involved in harassment, hateful conduct, or any form of manipulation or deceit.

Remember to always do some quick checks on an account before following it.

How to Mute an Account:

When you mute an account, tweets from that account will no longer appear in your feeds. This will not affect whether you follow each other. To mute, you can either:

- Open their Twitter profile, then click on the three dots beside the notification bell or follow/unfollow button.

- From the list of options, select **mute@username** to mute.

⌣ˣ Not interested in You might like

☺ Not interested in this Tweet

ಓ⁺ Follow @SenWhitehouse

🗒₊ Add/remove @SenWhitehouse from Lists

🔇 Mute @▓▓▓▓▓▓▓▓▓

⊘ Block @SenWhitehouse

</> Embed Tweet

⚐ Report Tweet

- A confirmation message will appear, click **"Yes, I'm sure"** to confirm.

Once an account is muted, their tweets and retweets will no longer be visible in your timeline, and you will no longer receive push or SMS notifications from that user. The muted user will still be able to favorite, reply to, and retweet your tweets; you just won't be notified of these activities.

Blocking Followers:

Blocking is a useful tool to prevent specific users from interacting with you on Twitter. You may block a follower If they send you abusive tweets or intentionally post offensive messages about you. Blocking a follower is a straightforward process:

- Go to the profile of the follower you wish to block.

- Tap the three dots icon (more icon) at the top of the profile.

- In the menu that appears, tap "**Block @user-name**."

- A confirmation message will appear, tap "**Block**" to confirm.

Once you block an account, they can't follow you or send you any messages, and you won't see their tweets or receive notifications about their activity. Remember, the blocked user isn't notified when you block them, but if they try to view your profile or interact with your tweets, they'll see they've been blocked.

CHAPTER SIX

Tweeting

You can compose your message or tweet, which is up to 280 characters. This will send your tweet into the timeline of your followers. In this chapter, you will learn how and what to tweet.

Deciding What To Tweet:

Deciding what to tweet on Twitter can sometimes be a challenge, particularly if you're new to the platform or if you're using it for business or professional purposes. Here are a few tips to guide you:

Identify Your Purpose: The content of your tweets will largely be determined by why you're on Twitter in the first place. Are you using it for personal, professional, or business purposes? Identifying your purpose will help guide your content.

Know Your Audience: Think about who your followers are or who you want them to be. What are they interested in? What kind of content do they typically engage with?

Share Useful Information: This could be news, insights, or facts related to your industry or areas of interest. This can establish you as a knowledgeable and helpful source of information.

Show Your Personality: Twitter is a social platform, so don't be afraid to be yourself. Share thoughts, opinions, and experiences that reflect who you are.

Use Visuals: Images, GIFs, and videos tend to get more engagement than text-only tweets. Use them to add interest to your tweets.

Remember, Twitter is a public platform, so think before you tweet. Make sure your tweets reflect your personal or professional brand and that they're likely to be of interest to your followers.

How to Create and Post Tweets:

Creating a tweet on Twitter is a straightforward process. Here's a step-by-step guide:

On Mobile App:

Open the Twitter app on your smartphone.

- Tap on the "**Compose**" button. This is usually represented by a blue circle with a white quill in it and can be found at the bottom right corner of the screen.

- You will see a text box that says "**What's happening?**" Tap there to start writing your tweet.

- You can add **photos**, **GIFs**, **polls**, or your **location** by tapping the relevant icons at the bottom of the compose box.

- Once you've written your tweet and added any desired elements, tap the "**Tweet**" button to post.

On Desktop (Twitter.com):

- Log in to your Twitter account on twitter.com.

- Click on the "**Tweet**" button. This is usually located in the left-hand menu bar.

- A pop-up window will appear with a text box that says "**What's happening?**" Click there to start writing your tweet.

- You can add **photos, GIFs, polls**, or your

location by clicking the relevant icons at the bottom of the compose box.

- Once you've written your tweet and added any desired elements, click the "**Tweet**" button to post.

NOTE: If you include a URL in your tweet, it will automatically be shortened to 23 characters, regardless of the actual length of the URL.

Twitter Threads:

A Twitter thread is a series of connected tweets posted by one user. It's a way to share more information or tell a longer story than can be accommodated in a single tweet due to Twitter's character limit. Here's how threads work:

(1) Creating a Thread: When composing a tweet, you have the option to add another tweet to it.

- On the Twitter app, select the "**Compose**" button (a blue circle with a white quill in it).

- Write your first tweet in the compose box.

- To create a thread, Tap the plus icon (+) to add another tweet to your thread. You can continue to add as many tweets as you need.

- Once you've finished writing your thread, tap the "**Tweet all**" button to post all the tweets in the thread at once.

(3) Posting a Thread: When you post a thread, all the tweets in the thread are posted at once, and they appear together in your followers' timelines. This means your followers can read the entire thread without having to visit your profile.

(4) Reading a Thread: When you see a tweet that is part of a thread, there will be a line connecting it to the subsequent tweet in the thread. You can click or tap "**Show this thread**" to read the entire thread.

Twitter Blue Tweet:

Twitter Blue subscribers can tweet up to 10,000 characters. This is a significant increase from the standard 280-character limit. This allows users to share longer stories, thoughts, and ideas.

It also makes it easier to share code, transcripts, and other types of content that are typically longer than 280 characters. In addition to the increased character limit, Twitter Blue subscribers also have access to other features, such as:

- The ability to customize their Twitter experience with themes and colors

- The ability to undo tweets

- The ability to save tweets for later

Conducting Twitter Poll:

Twitter polls are a great way to get feedback from your audience on a variety of topics. You can use polls to ask your audience about their thoughts on your content, your products or services, or even just their general opinions on current events. Here's how to conduct twitter poll:

- Open the Twitter app on your smartphone.

- Tap the "**Compose**" button, usually located at the bottom right corner of the screen.

- Tap the "**Poll**" icon, which looks like a bar chart, at the bottom of the compose box.

- Write your question in the main compose box. Then, fill in the options for your poll

where it says "**Choice 1**" and "**Choice 2**".
You can add up to four choices.

- Decide how long you want your poll to run.
  You can choose between 5 minutes or 7 days.

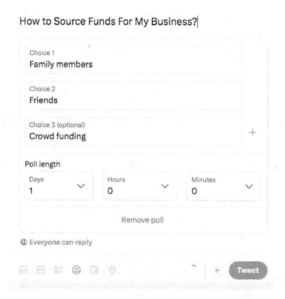

- Once you've set up your poll, tap "**Tweet**" to
  post it.

Here are some additional tips for conducting a Twitter poll:

- Time your poll for when your audience is most likely to be online.

- Keep your poll open for a reasonable amount of time, but not too long.

- Analyze the results of your poll and use them to improve your content and engagement.

Posting Videos on Twitter:

- Open the Twitter app on your smartphone.

- Tap the "**Compose**" button, and select the "**Gallery**" icon located at the bottom of the compose box.

- Choose a video from your device's gallery. You can trim the video to a desired length using the slider at the bottom.

- After you have chosen and trimmed your video, tap "**Done**" in the upper right corner.

- Write any accompanying text for your tweet in the compose box and select "**Tweet**" to post.

Creating Live Videos on Twitter:

From huge events to breaking news, you can find them all on Twitter. Using your Twitter account, you can quickly and simply produce live videos to broadcast in real time. Here is how to start a live video:

- Ensure to select the camera icon from the compose section

- The next step is to select "Live" from the menu.

- You can add location and description in the required field

- Select the Live button to start the streaming.

- Immediately your followers' timelines will be updated with the live broadcast.

NOTE: At any point, you can terminate a live video by clicking the Stop button in the upper left corner and then confirming your choice in the pop-up box.

Live Streaming with Third-Party Software:

Open up your streaming app settings: First, go to the settings area of the app or device you're using to stream. Look for something like "**Custom Streaming Server**" - this is where you're going to tell the app you want to stream to Twitter.

Pick Twitter as your streaming destination: There should be a dropdown menu or list of places you can stream to. Find "**Twitter**" in that list and select it. This tells the app that you want to stream on Twitter.

Sign in to your Twitter account: Now, you'll need to let the app access your Twitter account so it can send the stream there. It will ask you to log in to your

Twitter account, so just put in your username and password. Then it will ask if it's okay for the app to do things on your account - you'll need to say yes so it can stream your video.

Start your stream: Now that everything's set up, you can start streaming your video!

NOTE: These instructions should generally guide you, but different streaming apps might do things a bit differently.

Streaming From Other Social App to Twitter:

To post a real-time link for people to stream on Twitter, you need to have the stream set up on a platform that provides a shareable link, like YouTube, Twitch, or Facebook Live. Here are the steps:

1. **Set Up Your Stream:** First, you will need to set up your live stream on the platform you've chosen. Follow the platform's instructions to start a live stream.

2. **Get the Stream Link:** Once your live stream is ready, you'll need to get the shareable link. This will typically be available in the sharing options provided by your streaming platform.

3. **Share the Link on Twitter:** Go to Twitter and start composing a new tweet. Paste the link you copied from your streaming platform into the tweet. You can also add a description or comment to provide context to your followers.

4. **Post Your Tweet:** Once you're happy with the text and the link, click the "**Tweet**" button to post. Now, your followers will be able to click on this link to watch your live stream.

Remember to consider the time zones of your audience when scheduling your live stream. Providing some advance notice or scheduling a few reminder tweets can help ensure maximum viewer turnout.

Using Hashtag:

A hashtag on Twitter is any word or phrase immediately followed by the pound (#) sign. It allows Twitter to group all the tweets that contain that hashtag together, making it easy for users to find and follow discussions about particular topics. Here's how it works:

Creation: Anyone can create a hashtag by simply adding a "#" in front of a word or phrase without any spaces. For example, #TwitterTips, #Goodmusic, or #Apple.

Usage: When you include a hashtag in your tweet, it becomes a clickable link. When you click on it, you're taken to a search results page that displays all the tweets containing that hashtag. Tweets are displayed in real-time, meaning the most recent tweets appear at the top.

Discoverability: Hashtags help make your tweets discoverable to people who are interested in the topic. Even people who don't follow you can find your tweets through hashtags.

Trending Topics: Twitter identifies the most commonly used hashtags and displays them in the **"Trending"** section. Trending topics are determined based on a combination of the most popular current hashtags and a user's location.

Events and Campaigns: Hashtags are commonly used during events, conferences, TV shows, or marketing campaigns to gather all related discussions in one place.

Conversation: They also help in creating a conversation around a specific topic, where users participate by including the specific hashtag in their tweets.

Just remember to use hashtags judiciously. Using too many in one tweet can be counterproductive, as it can make your tweet difficult to read and can potentially come across as spammy.

Deleting Tweets

You can delete your tweets in a few simple steps

- Find the tweet either in your feed or in your profile

- Click the three dots at the upper right side of the tweet

- From the options, select *delete.*

CHAPTER SEVEN
Responding To Tweets

Engagement is a critical aspect of any social media platform, Twitter being no exception. Responding to tweets can increase visibility, facilitate networking, and enable you to manage your online reputation effectively. This chapter will teach you how to respond to tweets.

Responding to Tweets:

Responding to tweets allows you to engage directly with the person who posted the tweet. After reading a tweet or threads, you can craft an effective response to the tweeter. Here is how to go about it:

- **Read the Tweet:** In your timeline, locate and read the tweet or thread.

- **Click the Reply Icon:** Underneath the tweet, you'll find a few different icons. The one on the left, which looks like a speech bubble, is the reply icon. Click on it to start writing your comment.

Our Investing in America agenda is unleashing a Made-in-America innovation boom.

2:05 PM · May 27, 2023 · **362.9K** Views

557 Retweets   **79** Quotes   **2,881** Likes   **13** Bookmarks

- **Compose Your Comment:** A new box will appear where you can type in your response. Remember to keep your comment within

Twitter's character limit.

- **Review and Post:** Before posting, take a moment to review your comment. Check for any spelling or grammar mistakes, and make sure your comment is clear and respectful. Once you're happy with your comment, press the "**Reply**" button to post it.

NOTE: Your comment will then appear under the tweet and will also show up on your profile under the "**Tweets & Replies**" tab.

Retweeting:

A retweet is when someone shares someone else's tweet onto their own timeline. It's a way to quickly share interesting or relevant content with your own followers. Essentially, it's Twitter's version of a share or a repost.

When you retweet something, all of your followers can see that tweet in their timeline. This means that the reach of the original tweet is expanded. If many people retweet the same post, it can potentially be seen by millions of users, even if the original poster only had a small number of followers.

Retweeting is one of the primary ways that information, ideas, memes, and trends spread quickly on Twitter. It's a central part of the virality that characterizes the platform. Because of the ease and speed of retweeting, messages can spread rapidly across the globe.

When lots of people start retweeting the same hashtag or talking about the same subject, it can start to trend. However, a high volume of retweets alone doesn't guarantee a topic will trend. Here's how you can retweet someone's tweet:

- **Find the Tweet:** Scroll through your timeline or visit the profile of the person whose tweet you want to retweet. Locate the tweet you want to share.

- **Click the Retweet Icon:** Underneath the tweet, you'll find a few different icons. The second one from the left, which looks like two arrows forming a square, is the retweet icon. Click on it. You'll then have two options: **"Retweet"** and "**Quote Tweet**."

- **Choose How to Retweet:** If you just want to share the tweet without adding any comments of your own, click "**Retweet**." The tweet will then be shared with your followers. If you want to add a comment to the tweet, click "**Quote Tweet**." A text box will appear where you can type in your comment. After typing your comment, press the "**Tweet**" button.

Likes:

Like is a way to show appreciation for a tweet. It is a quick and easy way to show that you found a tweet interesting, amusing, or helpful. To like a tweet, you click on the heart-shaped icon underneath the tweet. This turns the icon red, showing that you have liked the tweet.

When you like a tweet, a couple of things happen:

Visibility: The tweet's author receives a notification that you've liked their tweet. It also shows up in your list of liked tweets, which others can see if they visit your profile and click on **Likes**.

Algorithm Influence: Twitter's algorithm uses likes as one of the factors when deciding what content to show in your feed and in other users' feeds.

The more likes a tweet gets, the more likely Twitter is to consider it interesting content and promote it to others.

Potential for Trending: If a tweet receives a large number of likes in a short period, it could contribute to making a particular subject trend on Twitter.

Share Tweet:

Sharing a tweet refers to the act of disseminating a tweet beyond its original audience without sharing it on my timeline. To share a tweet, simply select the "**Share**" option at the bottom of the tweet.

Here, you will find several ways to share the tweet:

Copy Link To Tweet: If you select this option, Twitter will generate a URL for the tweet and you can then paste the link wherever you like— in an email, a text message, a different social media platform, a blog post, and so on.

Share via Direct Message: If you want to share a tweet privately with another Twitter user, you can do so via Direct Message (DM). Here, you'll can select the recipient, send them the tweet privately.

Bookmark:

Bookmarking a tweet is a useful feature that allows you to save tweets for later reference without having to like them or retweet them. This is especially handy when you come across a tweet that you find interesting, but you don't have time to fully engage with it at that moment. Here's how to bookmark a tweet:

- **Find the Tweet:** Navigate to the tweet you want to bookmark.

- **Open the Share Menu:** In the bottom right corner of the tweet, you will find a share icon. Click on it to open its options.

- In the menu that appears, select the option **Add Tweet to Bookmarks.**

The tweet is now saved in your bookmarks. If you want to view your bookmarked tweets later, follow these steps:

- **Open the Side Menu:** On the Twitter app, tap on your profile picture at the top left corner of the screen to open the side menu.

- **Select Bookmarks:** In the menu, tap or click on **Bookmarks**. You will be taken to a list of all the tweets you've bookmarked.

Remember, your bookmarks are private. No one else can see what tweets you've bookmarked, unlike retweets or likes which are public.

Mute a Tweet:

Twitter allows you to mute specific tweets, meaning that you won't receive any more notifications about them. This can be particularly useful if a tweet you posted or interacted with has received a lot of attention and the constant notifications are becoming disruptive. Here's how to mute a tweet:

- Navigate to the tweet that you want to mute.

- Click on the "More" option located at the top-right corner of the tweet.

- From the menu that appears, select "**Mute @username**"

Once a tweet is muted, you'll no longer receive a tweet from the person who tweeted the message.

Blocking on Twitter:

Blocking is a more severe measure that can be used if another user is bothering you. When you block a user, they are no longer able to follow you, see your tweets, or interact with you through replies or direct messages. Here's how to block someone:

- Navigate to the profile of the person you want to block or from the person's tweet.

- Click on the three-dotted icon (on mobile) or the more icon (on desktop) located on their profile.

- Select "**Block @username**" and confirm your decision in the pop-up box.

Reporting a Tweet:

Reporting a tweet is the appropriate action to take if you come across content that violates Twitter's rules, such as hate speech, harassment, or explicit content. Here's how to report a tweet:

- Navigate to the tweet you want to report.

- Click on the down arrow at the top-right corner of the tweet.

- Select "**Report Tweet**" and follow the prompts to specify what kind of issue you're reporting (e.g It's abusive or harmful, It's spam, etc.)

- Provide any additional details as requested, then submit your report.

Twitter reviews reported tweets and takes appropriate action, which can range from issuing a warning to the offending user, requiring them to delete the violating tweet, temporarily limiting their account functionality, or suspending their account altogether.

CHAPTER EIGHT

Twitter Blue Subscription

Twitter Blue is a subscription-based service that Twitter introduced to provide its users with additional and unique features beyond the free-to-use version of the platform. In this chapter, you will learn more about Twitter Blue subscription.

Features of Twitter Blue:

Some of the features that Twitter blue offers subscribers are:

1. **Verification Checkmark:** To be eligible for verification as a Twitter Blue subscriber you

must meet the following criteria: Your account must be active for at least 90 days old with a verified phone number. Once an account meets these criteria, it will be automatically verified and will receive a blue checkmark.

2. **Undo tweets**: Twitter users have long asked for the ability to edit tweets after posting them. Twitter blue allows users to edit or delete tweets within a short while after they are first posted.

3. **Half Ads:** Twitter Blue subscriber has 50 percent less advertisement on the For You and Following feeds (timeline).

4. **Increased Rankings:** Your response in oth-

er people's Tweets or searches will be among the top or increase in ranking. In addition, all replies, mentions, and interactions from Twitter Blue users will appear in the Verified section of other users' alerts.

5. **Longer Tweets:** Twitter Blue subscribers can Tweet up to 10,000 characters. With this feature you can create lengthier Tweets for your followers or readers.

6. **Text formatting:** This feature is only available for twitter blue subscribers who are using the web version of twitter. This feature allows them to format text by bolding or italicizing the text.

7. **Bookmark Folders:** This feature allows

Twitter Blue subscribers to categorize their bookmark tweet into different folders for easy access. In addition, you can create as many folders and add different bookmark tweets of your choice.

8. **Custom Navigation:** This allows you to customize the bar at the bottom of the Twitter interface. You can remove or replace the default contents of the navigation bar. Any item you remove from the navigation bar is added to the sidebar/profile menu. You can also add new items up to a maximum of six.

9. **Custom app icons:** This feature is only available on Twitter app users. This feature helps twitter Blue subscribers to customize

the color of twitter app icon for a completely resigned look and feel.

10. **Longer video uploads:** This relatively new feature allows Twitter blue subscribers to post larger file size (8GB) and longer video content, up to two hours. This is a major improvement over the 200 seconds video limit for free Twitter users.

11. **Two-factor Authentication:** This is a security feature to protect your twitter account. You can add an extra layer of protection with instant authentication via SMS.

12. **Top Articles:** You may quickly see the most-read items in your social network by clicking on Top items. To help you quick-

ly identify relevant material, this function compiles a list of the most-shared articles from the accounts you follow, as well as the accounts they follow.

13. **Reader:** Make reading lengthy discussions more enjoyable.Twitter Blue subscribers have less background noise as they read lengthy threads. By tapping the reader symbol at the top of the thread, you can activate this feature as well as adjust the font size.

14. **Undo Tweet:** The Undo Tweet feature allows you to delete a Tweet after you've sent it, but before it becomes public. There is no actual "edit" button, but you may examine and change your Tweet before it becomes

public.

15. **Customized Theme:** You can customize your Twitter timeline by choosing a different color theme for your page. This is another benefit that is only available for Twitter blue subscribers.

Other Features of Twitter Blue include NFT Profile Pictures, Spaces Tab, and Twitter blue labs.

How to Subscribe Twitter blue

If you want to subscribe for Twitter blue here is how to go about the process:

- Log in to your Twitter account

- Tap on the profile icon at the top left to open the sidebar

- From the options, select *"Twitter Blue."*

- Select the Price of the subscription.

- Follow the prompt and add your payment details on the pop-up.

How to Pause & Cancel Twitter Blue

If you subscribe to Twitter blue and decide it's not for you, you have to cancel the subscription. If you fail to do so, the subscription will be renewed automatically when it expires.

To cancel your Twitter blue subscription:

- Log in to your Twitter account

- Tap on the profile icon at the top left to open the sidebar

- From the options, select *'Twitter blue.'*

- Select the option 'cancel subscription.'

- Confirm cancellation on the pop-up

Note that you can only cancel your Twitter blue subscription via the same channel you subscribed to - for example, Twitter for iOS, Twitter for Android, or the web version.

FAQ On Twitter blue

Here are a few commonly asked questions about Twitter blue that are not previously covered.

1. Can one get refunds on Twitter blue subscriptions?

Answer: No. All Twitter blue subscription payments are strictly non-refundable.

2. Does Twitter blue grant subscribers to dedicated customer support or faster support services?

Answer: The answer to this is not so simple. Twitter does offer dedicated support for issues pertaining to Twitter blue subscriptions and features. However, in general, issues pertaining to Twitter are handled by the regular Twitter support services, and there is no preference shown to Twitter blue subscribers in these.

3. Will Twitter become a paid platform?

Answer: No. Currently, Twitter blue is only available in four countries, and subscribers make up only a small number of the total Twitter users. So no, free Twitter isn't going anywhere any time soon.

4. Does Twitter blue offer free trials?

Answer: No, there is no free trial of twitter blue.

CHAPTER NINE

Trends & Search

Twitter Trends refer to the topics, hashtags, or keywords that are currently popular and widely discussed on the Twitter platform. In this chapter, you will learn more about Trends and how to use the Twitter search icon.

Twitter Trends:

Twitter Trends represent the most relevant and engaging conversations happening at a particular moment, providing users with a snapshot of what people are talking about in real-time.

The Twitter Trends section displays a list of the top trending topics or hashtags, usually customized based on your location and interests.

These trends are determined by Twitter's algorithm, which takes into account factors such as the volume of tweets, engagement, and the speed at which a topic is gaining popularity.

By clicking on a trend, you can explore the related tweets, media, and discussions happening around that particular topic. This allows users to join the conversation, share their thoughts, or discover new perspectives on a wide range of subjects—from breaking news and current events to entertainment, sports, and cultural moments.

Twitter Trends provide a valuable way to stay informed, discover new content, and engage with others on the platform. They serve as a window into the most relevant and popular conversations happening globally or within your specific location.

It's important to note that Twitter Trends can change frequently as new topics emerge and gain traction, reflecting the dynamic nature of the platform and the real-time nature of conversations on Twitter.

How to Make Your Tweet Go Viral:

Making a tweet go viral is not an exact science, as it depends on various factors and often involves an element of luck. However, here are some strategies that can increase the chances of your tweet gaining traction and potentially going viral:

Compelling Content: Create engaging and compelling content that resonates with your target audience. This could be a witty remark, a thought-provoking statement, a captivating image, or a humorous video. The key is to make it unique, interesting, and share-worthy.

Use Hashtags: Incorporate relevant and popular hashtags in your tweet to increase its discoverability. Hashtags help categorize your tweet and make it visible to a wider audience who may be searching or following those hashtags.

Timing is Key: Consider the timing of your tweet. Research shows that certain times of the day or week may be more favorable for maximum engagement.

Encourage Engagement: Ask questions, encourage retweets, or prompt users to share their thoughts and opinions. Engaging with your audience encourages participation and increases the likelihood of your tweet being shared or retweeted.

Tag Relevant Accounts: If your tweet mentions or is relevant to a specific person, brand, or organization, tag them in your tweet. This increases the chances of them seeing and potentially retweeting your content, expanding its reach.

Connect with Influencers: Engage with influencers or individuals who have a large following in your industry. If they find your content valuable or interesting, they may retweet or share it with their audience, giving your tweet more exposure.

Leverage Trending Topics: Keep an eye on trending topics and find ways to incorporate them into your tweets, as long as they are relevant to your brand or content. Participating in popular conversations can increase your tweet's visibility and potential for virality.

Remember, while these strategies can increase the chances of your tweet going viral, there is no guaranteed formula. Creating quality content and engaging with your audience consistently is key to building a strong presence on Twitter.

Local vs Global Trends:

Local trends and global trends on Twitter refer to the different sets of trending topics that are specific to a particular geographical location or have a broader, worldwide appeal. Here's an explanation of local trends and global trends:

Local Trends:

Local trends are specific to a particular geographic location, such as a city, region, or country.

- Twitter tailors these trends based on the user's location settings or IP address.

- Local trends allow users to discover what topics are currently popular and being discussed within their specific area.

- They provide a more localized perspective on conversations and events that are relevant to a particular location.

- Local trends include local news, events, or cultural phenomena gaining attention in a region.

Global Trends:

Global trends represent the most popular and widely discussed topics on Twitter worldwide.

- These trends are not limited to a specific location and are often of interest to a broad audience across different countries and regions.

- Global trends give users a sense of the trending conversations and viral topics that are capturing global attention.

- They can include international news, popular hashtags, viral memes, significant events, or trending discussions on a global scale.

- Global trends provide a broader view of the most engaging and popular content being shared and discussed on Twitter.

Users have the option to view either local trends or global trends depending on their preferences. The choice between local and global trends allows users to stay informed about both local and global conversations happening on the platform.

How to View Trending Topics:

To view and access trending topics on Twitter, follow these steps:

- On the Twitter homepage, click the "**Explore**" icon. It is represented by a magnifying glass symbol.

- In the Explore section, you will find a list of trending topics on the left-hand side or in the main feed.

- The trending topics are usually presented with a hashtag (#) and a brief description or a popular keyword or phrase.

- Scroll through the list to see the current trending topics.

- You can click on a specific trend to view the related tweets and join the conversation.

NOTE: Twitter may personalize the trending topics based on your location, interests, or the people you follow, providing you with a more tailored trending list.

Engaging with Trending Topics:

Engaging with trending topics on Twitter allows you to participate in popular conversations, share your thoughts, and connect with others who are discussing similar interests. Here are some ways to engage effectively with trending topics:

Understand the Context: Before joining a conversation around a trending topic, take the time to understand the context and background of the discussion. Read the related tweets, articles, or news to familiarize yourself with the topic's nuances.

Reply to Tweets: Reply to tweets from others who are discussing the trending topic. Engage in respectful and meaningful conversations. Ask questions, offer support, or share additional insights to foster engagement and build connections.

Use Relevant Hashtags: Incorporate relevant hashtags related to the trending topic in your tweets. This helps your tweets be more discoverable and increases the chances of others engaging with your content.

Follow Influencers: Follow influencers or thought leaders who are actively discussing the trending topic. Engage with their tweets to expand your reach and connect with their audience.

Twitter Search:

Twitter Search is a powerful feature that allows users to find specific content, tweets, accounts, or conversations on the platform. It enables users to explore a vast amount of real-time information and stay updated on topics of interest. Here's an explanation of Twitter Search and how to use it effectively:

Accessing Twitter Search: Select the search icon at the bottom of the Twitter homepage. The next step is to tap the search bar and enter the search terms.

Searching for Keywords or Hashtags: Enter your desired keywords, phrases, or hashtags in the search bar. You can search for topics, events, accounts, specific users, or even specific tweets. Twitter's search algorithm will display relevant results based on your search query.

Filtering Search Results: Twitter provides options to filter search results. You can filter by top tweets, latest tweets, accounts, photos, videos, news, and more. These filters help you find the most relevant content based on your preferences.

Advanced Search Filters: Twitter's advanced search settings provide additional filters to refine your search results. These filters include language preferences, date ranges, location, and more. Advanced search can help you narrow down your search to specific criteria.

Saved Searches: Twitter allows users to save their frequently used or favorite searches for quick access. Once you perform a search, click on the three-dot menu icon at the top-right of the search results and select "Save search" to save it for future use.

Exploring Trends and Moments: On the Twitter homepage or Explore section, you can find trending topics and Moments, which are curated collections of tweets related to specific events or stories. Clicking on a trend or Moment allows you to explore the relevant tweets and join the conversation.

How to Search for Accounts:

You can search for specific Twitter accounts by entering the username in the search bar. This allows you to quickly find and access a specific user's profile and view their tweets.

CHAPTER TEN

Subscriptions Creators

Twitter subscriptions allow users to earn money each month by sharing their content. When you have a subscription, your most dedicated followers can pay a fee to get special access and bonus content. In this chapter, you will learn about subscriptions.

As a creator, you have the opportunity to earn a portion of the money that Twitter makes from these subscriptions. Creators from around the world who meet certain requirements can apply to be part of the Subscriptions program.

Features Available in Subscriptions:

Here are the features that are available in subscriptions for creators:

Exclusive Tweets: Imagine having the power to share special tweets exclusively with your Subscribers. With Subscriptions, you can offer unique content that only your Subscribers get to see. It's like having a VIP club where you can share behind-the-scenes stories, exclusive announcements, or bonus content specifically for your most dedicated followers.

Subscriber Badge: When your Subscribers interact with you by replying to your tweets, they will have a distinctive badge displayed next to their username. This badge serves as a public symbol that showcases their status as your loyal Subscribers. It's a great way for you and others to identify and appreciate your dedicated audience members.

Subscribers Tab: Within your Notifications timeline, you will find a dedicated Subscribers Tab (currently available on iOS only). This special section provides you with an organized view of activities related to your Subscribers. It's like having a personal dashboard where you can easily keep track of your Subscriber community, their engagement, and respond to their interactions.

Subscription Links: To promote your Subscription offering and grow your audience, you'll have access to a unique link that directs people to your Subscription page. This link allows you to share information about your Subscription on Twitter and even outside the platform. You can include it in your bio, website, or other social media profiles, inviting people to become your Subscribers and enjoy exclusive content.

Subscriptions Community: As a Subscriptions creator, you'll be part of the official Subscriptions Creators Feedback Community on Twitter. This community is an exclusive space where you can connect and collaborate with fellow creators who are also using Subscriptions. It's a supportive network where you can share experiences, seek advice, and provide feedback to help shape the future of the Subscriptions feature.

Subscriber-only Spaces: Hosting live conversations is a fantastic way to engage with your audience. With Subscriptions, you can create subscriber-only Spaces, which are virtual rooms where only your

Subscribers can join and participate. This exclusive environment allows you to have focused discussions, Q&A sessions, or even organize special events for your loyal Subscribers.

Who can Participate as Subscriptions Creators?

Currently, Subscriptions Creators have the opportunity to sign up for the program on a global scale, provided that they are in countries supported by stripe and they meet the minimum eligibility criteria such as; An active Twitter user who is above 18 years and having at least 500 followers

To apply, you can easily submit an application directly from the main menu of your Twitter app. Here's how to:

- From the main menu in your Twitter app.

- Ensure to click **Monetization**.

- The next step is to click **Subscriptions**.

The application process is designed to identify creators who meet the necessary requirements and are a good fit for the Subscriptions program. If you are eligible and meet the criteria, your application will be considered for selection.

CHAPTER ELEVEN

Twitter Settings

In the ever-evolving world of social media, understanding and mastering the settings of your chosen platform is crucial. This chapter focuses on the various settings offered by Twitter and how you can control many aspects of your Twitter experience.

Your Account Settings:

Your Account settings is a section on Twitter where you can see information about your account. You can see the details you filled in when signing up for Twitter. Here is how to customize this feature:

- The first step is to select the **side menu** to reveal the option bar.

- The next step is to select "**Settings & Support**" from the options.

- In the drop-down menu, select "**Settings and Privacy**."

- The next step is to select "**Your Account**" from the option. In this section, you can customize the following:

Account Information: In this section, you will see your account information, such as username, phone number, email address, country, and automation. You can select any of the sections to customize or edit.

Change Password: In this section, you can change your Twitter account password.

Download an Archive of your Data: In this section, you will be able to download information that has been stored for your account.

Deactivate Account: In this section, you will begin the process of deactivating your account. It is important to note that once your account has been deactivated, every information about your account will be deleted from the platform.

Security and Account Access:

Security and account access is a section in Twitter where you can manage the security of your account usage and apps connected to your Twitter account. Here is how to customize this feature:

- The first step is to select the **side menu** to reveal the option bar.

- The next step is to select "**Settings & Support**" from the options.

- In the drop-down menu, select "**Settings and Privacy**."

- The next step is to select "**Security and Account Access**" from the option. In this section, you can customize the following:

Security: In this section, you can customize the security of your Twitter account by enabling two-factor authentication with text message or authenticator app. You can also enable additional password protection.

Apps Session: This section will provide information about third-party apps connected to your account. You will also see your Twitter logged-in devices and account access history.

Connected Account: In this section, you will see social accounts that are connected to your Twitter account. For example, if you use Google to sign up on Twitter, it will be connected to your Twitter account.

Privacy and Safety:

In this section, you will be able to manage the information you see and interact with on Twitter. Here is how to customize this feature:

- The first step is to select the **side menu** to reveal the option bar.

- The next step is to select **"Settings & Support"** from the options.

- In the drop-down menu, select **"Settings and Privacy."**

- The next step is to select **"Privacy and Safety"** from the option. In this section, you can customize the following:

Audience and Tagging: Here, you can manage the information other people can see on Twitter. In this section, you will be able to enable "**Protect Tweet**" as well as "**Photo Tagging**."

Your Tweet: Here, you will be able to manage information associated with your tweet. You can enable Twitter to mark your tweet as containing material that may be sensitive.

Content You See: In this section, you will be able to customize the tweet that you see from other users. You can decide the topics, interests and explore settings based on your preference.

Mute and Block: In this section, you can manage the Twitter account you have muted or blocked. Also, in this section, you will be able to add muted words, and you will not get any notifications for tweets that include such words.

Direct Message: In this section, you can manage people who can send you direct messages on Twitter. You can also enable certain features such as "**Read Receipt**" and "**Message Request**."

Spaces: In this section, you will be able to manage your space activities. You will be able to customize your followers to see which spaces you are listening to. Also, you will be able to manage your space recording history.

Discoverability and Contacts: In this section, you will be able to control your Twitter account discoverability and manage contacts you have imported to Twitter. Here, you can enable whether you want others to find you by mail or Phone number.

Notification Settings:

The notification setting allows you to customize how Twitter should notify you concerning information concerning your account. Here is how to access this settings:

- The first step is to select the **side menu** to reveal the option bar.

- The next step is to select **"Settings & Support"** from the options.

- In the drop-down menu, select **"Settings and Privacy."**

- The next step is to select **"Notification"**

from the option. In this section, you can customize the following:

Filters: Here, you can choose the notifications you want to see and the tweets you won't see. For example, muted notifications are where you can customize notifications from people.

Preference: Here, you can select your preferences that you want notifications from. This is where you can enable "**unread notification count badge**" and customize "**push notifications.**"

Accessibility Settings:

Accessibility settings are designed to make Twitter more usable for individuals with different abilities: Here is how to customize this feature:

- The first step is to select the **side menu** to reveal the option bar.

- The next step is to select "**Settings & Support**" from the options.

- In the drop-down menu, select "**Settings and Privacy**."

- The next step is to select "**Accessibility, display and languages**" from the option.

- Ensure to select "**Accessibility**" to customize the following:

Screen Reader: Here, you can enable Pronounce # as hashtag.

Motion: Here, you can enable as well as customize

"**Reduced Motion**" and "**Video autoplay**."

Media: You can enable a setting that allows you to add descriptions, also known as alt-text, to images in Tweets. This can make images more accessible for people using screen readers or those who have low-bandwidth connections.

Gesture: Here you can add the ability to tap on the explore tab icon to start searching.

Display and Sound:

Display and sound settings in Twitter is where you can customize how your Twitter timeline displays images as well as play certain media when using the app. Here is how to customize this feature:

- The first step is to select the **side menu** to reveal the option bar.

- The next step is to select **"Settings & Support"** from the options.

- In the drop-down menu, select **"Settings and Privacy."**

- The next step is to select **"Accessibility, display and languages"** from the option.

- Ensure to select "**Display**" to customize the following:

Media Preview: This setting controls whether images and videos in your Twitter feed are automatically previewed. If you turn this on, you'll see media directly in your feed. If you turn it off, you'll only see media if you click on a tweet to expand it.

Dark Mode: Twitter offers a "Dark Mode" that changes the color scheme of the platform to darker colors. This can be easier on your eyes in low light environments and may save battery life on some devices. You can choose to have it always on, use it only in low light conditions, or switch it on and off manually.

Sound Effects: These settings control the sounds

your device makes when you interact with Twitter. For instance, you might hear a sound when you refresh your feed or send a tweet. You can turn these sounds on or off based on your preference.

Use In-app Browser: This setting determines how links in tweets are opened. If this setting is enabled, links will open within the Twitter app itself using Twitter's built-in browser. If you disable this setting, links will open in your device's default web browser instead.

Customizing Twitter Data Usage:

Twitter gives users the ability to manage and customize their data usage settings. These settings allow you to control how much data Twitter uses on your device, particularly useful when you're on a metered or limited data plan. Here is how to customize this feature:

- The first step is to select the **side menu** to reveal the option bar.

- The next step is to select **"Settings & Support"** from the options.

- In the drop-down menu, select **"Settings and Privacy."**

- The next step is to select **"Accessibility, dis-**

play and languages" from the option.

- Ensure to select "**Data Usage**" to customize the following:

Data Saver: If enabled, this setting reduces the amount of mobile data Twitter uses by not automatically loading images in high quality or autoplaying videos.

High-quality Images: This setting, when turned on, allows Twitter to load images in higher quality. If you're concerned about data usage, you might want to use this only over Wi-Fi.

High-quality Image Uploads: This allows you to upload images in higher quality. Again, depending on your data plan, you might want to limit this to when you're connected to Wi-Fi.

High-quality Video: Similar to the high-quality images setting, enabling this will allow Twitter to load videos in higher quality.

High-quality Video Uploads: This setting allows you to upload videos in higher quality. Keep in mind that uploading high-quality videos might consume more data.

Video Autoplay: This setting controls whether videos automatically start playing as you scroll through your feed. You can usually set this to play automatically always, never, or only when connected to Wi-Fi.

CHAPTER TWELVE
Advance Tips and Tricks

This chapter provides guidance on how to personalize your Twitter account through various tips and tricks. By following these tips, you can improve your skills and knowledge on using Twitter, which may lead to becoming an expert in the platform. Let us begin now.

Everything About Twitter Space:

Twitter Spaces is a feature introduced by Twitter that allows users to host and participate in live, audio-only conversations. Here's how Twitter Space works:

How to start a Twitter Space:

- Open the Twitter app on your smartphone.

- Proceed to select the **"Twitter Space"** icon at the bottom.

- Tap on the "+" icon within the Spaces section at the bottom of your screen. Alternatively, you can long press the compose tweet button and tap on the Spaces icon.

- Add a name or description for your Space.

- Ensure to tap **"Start your Space."**

How to invite people to your Twitter Space:

When you create a Space, you have the option to invite others to join it. One way to invite others to join a Space is by sharing a link to it or by sending out an invitation through a tweet. In a Space, you have the option to send direct invites to listeners. To invite people to speak during a conversation, you can tap on the "**Invite to speak**" icon and choose the individuals you wish to invite.

Roles within a Twitter Space:

- **Host:** A host is the individual who initiates a Space. In a Space, the host has the ability to manage the speakers and can also remove individuals from the Space if necessary. It is possible for a host to designate co-hosts to assist in managing the Space.

- **Co-host:** A co-host is a participant in a Space who has been granted the same privileges as the host, with the exception of the ability to end the Space or remove the host.

- **Speaker:** Speakers are individuals who have the ability to communicate verbally in a given setting, including in a space or room. In a virtual event, the host has the ability to extend an invitation to individuals to become speakers. Additionally, listeners have the option to request to speak during the event.

- **Listener:** A listener is someone who is present in a particular space or setting but does not have the ability to speak or participate in the conversation or activity. In a virtual space, users have various options to engage with the content. They can express their reactions to what they hear by using emojis, access important information by reading any pinned Tweets, follow along with captions, actively participate by Tweeting about the Space, or request to speak and join the conversation.

Twitter Space Tips:

- **Reactions:** Listeners and speakers can react to what they hear using emojis.

- **Pinned Tweets:** The host can pin Tweets to the Space. These will be visible to all participants.

- **Captions:** Spaces uses live captioning to make the conversation more accessible. This can be turned on or off in the settings.

How to Filter Tweets

Customizing Tweet filters is important to enhance your Twitter experience. The content we see online can have a significant impact on our mood, outlook, and overall digital experience. Here is how to customize the filtering of your Tweets:

- Proceed to the *"More Option"*

- Scroll down and tap *"Setting and Privacy"*

- The next step is to tap *"Notification"*

- Then, tap *"Filter"*

- Ensure to check the box of *"Quality filter"*

How to Add Location to your Tweet

Adding a location to your tweets can provide context to your messages and let your followers know where you are tweeting from. This can be especially useful if you are attending a specific event, like a concert or a conference, and you want to share that experience with your followers. Here's how you can add a location to your tweet:

- **Start a new tweet:** Click on the 'Tweet' button to start composing a new message.

- **Click on Location:** Depending on the device you're using, there should be a location icon or an option to add a location near the text box where you're composing your tweet.

- **Choose a location:** You can search for a specific location or select one from the suggestions provided.

- **Post your tweet:** Once you've added your desired location, you can finish composing your tweet and click 'Tweet' to post it.

Running Twitter Ads:

Running Twitter ads is a great way to reach a larger audience, promote your brand or products, and drive engagement on the platform. Here's a general step-by-step guide on how to run Twitter ads:

Set Up a Twitter Ads Account: To set up a Twitter Ads account, you need to visit the Twitter Ads website at ads.twitter.com. You can either sign in using your existing Twitter account or create a new account specifically for advertising purposes.

Choose Your Campaign Objective: When creating a campaign, it is important to choose a specific objective that you want to achieve. This will help you to focus your efforts and measure the success of your campaign. Some common campaign objectives include increasing brand awareness, generating leads, driving website traffic, and boosting sales. This will help you to focus your efforts and ensure that your campaign is effective in achieving the desired outcome.

Define Your Target Audience: Defining your target audience means identifying the specific group of people who are most likely to be interested in your product or service. Twitter provides a range of targeting options that enable you to reach your desired audience. These options include demographics, interests, behaviors, keywords, and even specific accounts or events.

Set Your Campaign Budget: When creating a marketing campaign, it is important to set a budget for it. This budget will determine how much money you are willing to spend on advertising, promotions, and other marketing activities. By setting a budget, you can ensure that you are not overspending and that you are getting the most out of your marketing efforts.

Create Your Ad Content: When creating ad content, it's important to consider your target audience and the message you want to convey. Your ad should be clear, concise, and attention-grabbing. Use persuasive language and highlight the benefits of your product or service. Make sure to include a call to action that encourages viewers to take action, such as visiting your website or making a purchase.

Choose Ad Placements: When advertising on Twitter, it's important to select the appropriate ad placements. This means deciding where you want your ads to appear on the platform. Twitter offers different ad placements for advertisers to choose from, such as the Twitter timeline, search results, or within Twitter's Explore section.

Launch and Monitor Your Campaign: Launching and monitoring your campaign is an essential part of any marketing strategy. It involves setting up your campaign and keeping a close eye on its progress to ensure that it is meeting your goals. By doing so, you can make any necessary adjustments to improve its effectiveness and maximize your return on investment.

Analyze and Optimize: To improve the effectiveness of your Twitter ads, it's important to analyze and optimize their performance. You can achieve this by utilizing Twitter's analytics and reporting tools, which allow you to track the success of your ads and make data-driven decisions to improve their performance.

Authors Request

Dear Reader,

I hope this message finds you well. As an author, I am reaching out to you with a humble request for your support. Your feedback and reviews hold tremendous value, not only to me but also to potential readers who are contemplating purchasing my book.

Reviews play a pivotal role in aiding other readers to make informed decisions about whether my book is the perfect fit for them. Your honest opinions and personal experiences can provide invaluable insights into the content, writing style, and overall worth of the book.

By sharing your thoughts, you can assist others in gaining a better understanding of what to anticipate and whether it aligns with their interests and needs.

Moreover, your reviews serve as a wellspring of encouragement and motivation for me as an author. Knowing that my work has made an impact or resonated with readers fuels my passion and unwavering dedication to continue creating valuable content.

Taking just a few minutes of your time to leave a review on Amazon would mean the world to me, whether it's a brief comment about what you found helpful or a detailed explanation of your experience.

Your contribution will make a genuine difference, shaping the decisions of potential readers and supporting my ongoing efforts to deliver meaningful content.

Thank you in advance for your invaluable support, time, and feedback. Your reviews truly make a difference, and I am profoundly grateful for your continued support as I strive to deliver valuable content to readers like you.

Warmest regards,

Zara Greenwood

About the Author

Zara Greenwood is a passionate writer and social media enthusiast dedicated to helping individuals harness the power of Twitter. With her extensive experience in digital marketing and a deep understanding of social media dynamics, Zara has become a go-to expert for beginners looking to navigate Twitter.

Having started her own journey on Twitter as an absolute beginner, Zara knows the challenges and uncertainties of venturing into the world of social networking. Motivated by her own learning experiences, she set out to create a comprehensive guide that simplifies the complexities of Twitter for newcomers.

When she's not immersed in the world of social media, Zara enjoys exploring the outdoors, pursuing her passion for photography, and spending quality time with her family and friends. Connect with Zara Greenwood on Twitter (@ZaraGreenwood9) to receive updates on her latest projects.